MW01065395

A Journey Through Love And Peace of Mind

By Joe Vigil

True North House Publishing

True North House
publishing
worldwide

Worldwide

First Edition

ISBN: 978-0-359-45091-6

True North House Publishing

Worldwide

Please contact TrueNorthHouse@live.com before using any material from this book. Thank you.

Find Joe Vigil on Facebook: Facebook.com/6joevigil6

Cover design: Alexander Beat
www.AlexanderBeat.com

Photography: Jen Nachor
wickedesigner@gmail.com

Art: Everett Joens
Lostgalleries.com

ISBN 978-0-359-45091-6

90000

9 780359 450916

It was at the age of 13 that I first put pen to paper. I had a dream to become a rock star and my creativeness was just beginning. Inspired by my newfound liking of one Nikki Sixx, I was determined. Over the years as my talent grew, I realized it was easy to write about things that I saw happening in the world around me. Falling in love, feeling pain, current events, it didn't matter, I was able to express it through poetry. My rock star dreams never came true, but even better, I have been able to write in ways that have inspired and made people smile and feel better about the world they live in. I never thought that I would reach the day that I would share my stories, but here it is.

Through love, heartache, sadness, joy and happiness this is just a small part of my Journey Through Love to reach Peace of Mind. Every one of us is on some kind of Journey, we may be different in many ways but are alike in so many more.

This book is dedicated to the one person who has put up with my craziness and has kept me grounded through it all, Alissa. I Love You More Than You Know!

Thank you to everyone and everything that has given me the inspiration to write. Trust me when I say I am forever grateful. Some of these are indeed born from the inspiration you have given me in the time we have known each other. Alissa, Sebastian, Devlin and Gabriella Vigil, Jen Nachor, Everett Joens, Nikki Frazier, Mother Nature, Nikki Sixx, Marvin the Martian, My Mother Judy, Father Joe and my 4 sisters, Annette, Lisa, Lori and Christie. Floriano Trujillo, Chris @ The Kimo Theatre, Amy Biehl High School and The Cathedral Basilica of St. Francis Assisi.

It took decades of pushing by these people to finally inspire me to share with the world. So here it is, my Journey Through Love and Peace of Mind.

Joe

A Journey Through Love

We all have goals
Full of desires,
Thoughts within,
Fueling our fires,
We all have dreams,
From life anew,
Feelings from the heart,
To get us through,
Until the end,
Our need never fades,
Consuming our nights,
Fulfilling our days,
Along this path,
With guidance from above,
We make this trip,
On a journey through love.

The world will pass you by,
If you stand in the same place,
Like the sun dancing across the sky,
Each moment passed cannot be replaced,
Grab hold and step ahead,
Change only what makes you sad,
Live life without regret,
Don't get lost in what you had,
Something new always awaits,
New dreams to come true,
Reach out and seize the day,
Breathe and live for you.

Its light will blind you,
Its power will bind you,
Without caution you're sure to fall,
If you let it control you,
It is destined to throw you,
Into a realm of not knowing at all.

If you hold on to what you cannot have,
Pain is all you will feel,
It just takes time for your eyes to see,
What is fantasy and what is real,
Your heart is your core protect it well,
It's beat will light the way,
Never fall for devious intentions,
The truth will reveal itself one day,
Lessons learned is how we should live,
To gain strength for walking through sorrow,
Our tears are a shield that protects our souls,
With the promise of a better tomorrow.

I walk through life
My back turned to the wind,
Looking for ways to walk away,
Waiting for new dreams to begin,

The sun kisses me each morning
Without a hint of what's in store,
I embrace each new day
Just as I did before,

Winning is never easy,
Losing comes so free,
I smile and take another step
Towards what is good for me,

One day I'll wake to a brand new day
All doubts erased from sight,
I'll kiss the morning heart and soul
And believe everything's alright.

I've walked through dark places,
I've seen the light shine,
I've searched for answers to haunting questions,
Only to realize they subside in time,
I've hung my head low,
With tears acting as the anchor to my life,
Dragging me down to forbidden depths
Walking the sharpened edge of the knife,
I emerged with strength unrealized,
Found truth in what I feel,
To the darkness that harbors deep within my soul,
I shall no longer kneel,
I face each day with optimism,
I smile at life's daunting tasks,
I stand tall with heart and mind as one,
For I've conquered peace at last.

The reality of loss never quite sets in,
We adjust and learn to live another way,
As time passes, we seem to forget,
All those words we wished we could say,
Our hearts keep beating,
Just as they always have before,
Because somehow, you're still here,
Although together we can't laugh and cry no more,
When the sadness shows,
Upon our face,
Your hand reaches down,
And with love it is replaced,
When the will gives in,
When it becomes too much to bear,
Somehow, the sun still shines,
Somehow, you're still there,
With that I will smile,
Because no other strength will do,
I may have wished a million words,
But now I say Thank You,
Thank you for the memories,
For being strong enough to make it through,
For a love that knows no loss,
For being a part of me, Thank You.

As hard as it may seem,
When life gets you down,
Sometimes all you need,
Is to take a look around,
Loss may close your eyes,
Blind you with its pain,
Deep within your heart,
The strength will always remain,
You'll feel the desperation,
The selfishness from the mind,
But your heart will keep on beating,
And pick you back up when it's time,
The empty feeling will never fade,
In time memories will no longer bring pain,
A smile will replace never ending tears,
Once again the light will shine through the rain,
We'll see that we are surrounded,
By those giving love to lead the way,
Just look around with open heart,
Life starts anew today.

I hide behind your smile,
I hide behind your head held high,
I hide, but all the while,
A part of you has died,
I hide behind the sunshine,
I hide behind the rain,
I hide behind your words "I'm fine,"
Because that's what I do, I'm pain.

Dream a dream, a million dreams,
Nothing is ever as it seems,
A chapter of life on a subconscious screen,
Playing memories through a visual scene,
What once was lost has now returned,
Behind closed eyes for lessons not learned,
Heed the visions of what your mind sees,
Within darkest silence you'll find peace.

Addiction is the greed that fills,
The need inside your mind that kills,
The hope and dreams buried deep within,
Your eyes only to start over again,
One more time into the fire,
Burning away all that is desired,
By many yet touched by just a few,
A million times and then it's through,
A losing battle, strength be lost,
To your laughing devil your soul the cost,
Of the skeletons you hold inside,
Your mind you know can never hide,
Signed in blood resembling your name,
Spoken often but never the same,
Ending is all that is guaranteed,
To be the answer to your addictive greed,
Leaving behind pain in sorrow,
Behind the tears sure to fall tomorrow,
Will never come for those who knew,
What tomorrow could be like shared with you.

Touch the flame burning from a blackened desire,
Feel the power born from the fire,
Welcome inside the heat within,
Close your eyes let the dream begin,
Moving motionless time stands still,
Reaching out nothing to feel,
Screaming aloud no voice is heard,
Definition avoiding all the words,
Helplessly lost your welcome is found,
Willingly led without a sound,
Within the flames of the candles fire,
Lies the answer to what you desire.

The sun still shines
Within the world in which you live,
One step in front of the other
Giving all you have to give,
Darkened closets, searching for light
With the energy needed so far away,
With each breath upon the rising sun
You wonder how you'll make the day,
Don't bury the pain, let it be your strength
Through the fog it's hand will guide,
Beyond the tears that seem so endless
The path lies somewhere deep inside,
It's only you who can find the will
To find the passion this life bleeds,
Letting go is never forever
Yet it's needed to be free,
Say goodbye, but just for now
For tomorrow we do not know,
Peace only comes upon acceptance
It's needed for you to grow,
Missing is natural, as are the feelings inside
Let them heal your broken heart,
Hold the memories with all you have
With them you'll never be apart.

Look deep within the blue
Of the Heavenly sky above,
Beyond the polluted hatred
To find untarnished love,
Search deep inside the green
Of the mountain's towering pine,
To see the beauty of nature's mother
That seems so hard to find,
Walk beyond the banks of the river
Into her open arms,
To feel the peace she has to offer
To bathe in her natural charm,
Awaken deep within your heart
To free the freedom inside,
To feel this life in all its beauty
Your generous soul to be your guide,
Live past the tears of yesterday
Accept the buried sorrow,
A free mind, will help you find
The promises of tomorrow.

Starry night
Upon a darkened sky,
Mother Earth turns
As the moon waves goodbye,
Chaos ensues
Upon her land,
All of creation
Praying for God's helpful hand,
Brother versus brother
Humanity turns against its own,
A condemned realization
Of a species that has yet grown,
Hatred fills
All the elders eyes,
As fear takes over
All young lives,
Hope is not lost
With faith a dream shall rise,
Lay down your animosity
Give peace a try.

I judged a book by its cover,
Within its artwork I was elated,
As I looked inside, I discovered,
There was no story amongst its pages,
Although its makeup shouted pretty,
There was no substance deep inside,
For now my heart has pity,
Because in it I wished to confide,
Into the facade I was drawn,
With hope growing like a storm,
Played just like a pawn,
Now I stand here torn,
Should I lay it to collect dust,
From it just walk away,
A moment of shattered trust,
Imagination it shall not play,
A breath taken so deep,
I shall not be fooled again,
For this story I will not read,
Never knowing where it shall end.

I loved you yesterday,
I love you today,
Even still,
You take my breath away,
You are my reality,
You are my dream,
You are my life,
My everything,
Thank you, my love,
My Babydoll,
For giving your heart,
Giving me your all,
Our love is eternal,
Our time won't end,
My heart my soul,
My best friend,
I give you my love,
Tomorrow even more,
As each moment passes,
Even stronger than before.

Eternal Fear

If you could see inside my mind,
Or read the tears behind my eyes,
You'd be frightened by what you'll find,
You'd fall deaf by my silent cries,

If you could hold my heart in your hand,
Or be my life for just a day,
You'd feel the pain but not understand,
You'd move your lips with nothing to say,

If you could scream with all your might,
Or remain silent against your will,
You'd also want to quit the fight,
You'd lose control of what you feel,

If you could feel my pain inside,
Or watch my soul disappear,
You'd know the feelings I must hide,
You'd see my eternal fear.

Rain

Decisions to make inflicting pain,
Tears fall like never-ending rain,
Harmless intentions from the start,
Harmful actions ripping you apart,
Tomorrow comes a brand-new day,
Only your life is stuck in replay,
Running in circles gaining no ground,
A bleeding heart makes no sound,
A fictitious smile for the world to see,
The perfect mask for agony,
Believing in what you've made real,
Ignoring the truth in what you feel,
Beyond the pain in blinded eyes,
Louder than the silence behind your cries,
Someday the suns darkness will begin to fade,
A receipt given for life's dues paid,
The doors are open ready to walk through,
The first step is up to you,
No more standing in the rain,
No more drowning in the pain.

Her womb protected you then,
Her heart surrounds you today,
Forever your closest friend,
Never too far away,

Her shoulders are there for your tears,
Her arms to give embrace,
As a child she chased your fears,
Wiped the fear from your face,

She listens to your stories,
Hung pictures you first drew,
Her heart holds the memories,
From her first time feeling you,

Some may have a sister or brother,
Some may have some they never knew,
Nothing compares to the love a mother,
Will forever have for you.

Change

She sighs on the morning
That she suspects a change
Something's different about her
Her story has a new page
For so many years
She hoped and she prayed
She cried to the Heaven's
To let her dream live some day
Now she knows it's real
Finally, it is true
The blessing of nature
A life so brand new
She smiles in the mirror
As she watches her world change
Life and body take new form
Love grows in her heart each day.

New Life

A seed is planted
New life will start
From early on
Sincere love in her heart
So many changes
Anxiety runs high
Happiness of the miracle
Is seen in her eyes
A bond greater than all
Grows stronger each day
Nothing in this world
Will make this love go away
When the time comes
And nature says they must part
They'll be one for eternity
From the time new life starts.

My Love

I wished upon a star falling
To send an angel my way
Somehow, someway, she'd hear me calling
And come to me someday
The gods of love with open hearts
Will bring us to unite
Neither one more day to be apart
Nor another lonely night
I close my eyes and wish I do
To all the Heaven's above
And when they open, I see you
My friend, my life, my love

Imagination

Is there another world
To escape to
To live free
Is there another place
Where things
Can be what they may be
Maybe this world
Can be good
If we make it that way
But is there anyone
Out there willing
To give it the time or day

Are we evil creatures
Filled with hate
Will we ever change
Our world and our fate

Imagination come set me free
Imagination please rescue me
Imagination you're my only chance
Imagination we meet at last

Tales of Mr. Oak

He told me of the little boy
Who dug the hole and planted the seed
Of the man, who owned the plantation
All in the name of greed
The pretty belle who'd read her pages
Protected by his shade
The squirrels who hid their acorn nuts
As he watched the children play
The story that touched my heart the most
Was of the soldier who shed a tear
Dressed in gray, covered in dust
Had been fighting for almost a year
He asked why should brothers fight
For freedom when it should come free
Why must I hunt my own blood
As I know he hunts for me
He dried his eyes, said a prayer
Asking for peace to come someday
Said, if you see my brother, give him my love
And in the sunset, walked away.

Silent Cries

What's going on
Through your mind
What's the vision
In your eyes
Broken promises
Heartbreaking lies
Open up and let
The world hear you cry
Thoughts of giving up
Are circling in the air
You give your warning
No one seems to care
You need to escape
Run somewhere
There's no place
Without truth or dare
Dreams die
Birds no longer fly
In the lonely world
Of silent cries.

The Memory

Why is it your life can change
With just the blink of an eye
When someone so dear to your heart
Receives their call to fly
It makes your mind go blank
Your world slowly falls apart
Feels like you can't go on
You just can't make a new start
They're here forever in memory
As is their love within your heart
They'll hold the tears you cry
Shed light when your world dark
Hold on to the memory
Of the love you shared
Keep inside your heart
The feelings that were there
Although the one you love is gone
They're never too far away
So hold on to the memory
You'll be together again someday.

More Than You Know

On a lonely night
You came into my life
Took me by the heart
Showed me where to start
Now we'll never be apart

I love you more than you know
Oh how I love you so
Together our love will grow
More than you know

I'll take your hand
I'll be your man
Now and forever
We'll always be together
My life couldn't be better

The person you are inside
Are the reasons why
I'll never let you go
My love I'll always show
I love you more than you know.

Life is Unpredictable

Life is unpredictable
With surprises around each bend
One minute it crushes your heart
Then gives its love to help it mend
It's up to us to learn
The lessons it has to give
To cry our tears of sorrow
Gain the strength to help us live
Never take for granted
Or get buried beneath the walls
Life is unpredictable
Yet so precious to us all

Butterfly

I was walking through life
Pretending all I needed was mine
Somewhere deep inside
I knew a light had yet to shine
I've surfed atop the waves
Survived storms that came ashore
Sometimes feeling invincible
Thinking I needed nothing more
Now my thoughts are changing
My mind breaking new ground
A butterfly floating in the air
Towards my heart without a sound
Etched upon my memory
Consuming my thought throughout the day
Strange, but I know I'm sure
I don't want this butterfly to drift away
As Spring shows her beauty
Like butterflies born upon a fire
I'll grab hold with heart and soul
And soar with her higher…and higher

If I Could…I Would

If I could take away your pain,
I would
If I could blow away the rain,
I would
If I could shelter you fears,
I would
If I could stop the tears,
I would
If I could share my light,
I would
If I could help through another night,
I would
I know I can be there,
As you would
I could make you smile, show I care,
As you would
If I could help you through another day,
I would
If I could help your sadness go away,
I could…I would…I will

Yesterday Today

Yesterday I seen not what tomorrow holds
But today I watch as yesterday unfolds

This morning I seen the light
Now all is blinded
Will tonight replace today
This morning my thoughts were blank
Now they're desperate and murky
Tonight will I dream them away

In the past I was alone
The present I feel so scared
In the future I'll find someone new
The past brings back memories
The present brings new love
In the future I will still think of you

Yesterday the sky was clear
Today the clouds roll in
Tomorrow will bring the rain
Yesterday you were by my side
Today I'm all alone
Tomorrow is when I will feel the pain

Goodbye

Sadly all know
In a mere second of life
A time to say goodbye
A love once known
Suddenly is gone
Passing with a cry
To let go is hard
Forgetting is impossible
No matter how much you try
When something is missing
Gone forever
So hard to say goodbye

No More the Children Cry

From a high school letterman
To a Gulf War Veteran
The mental anguish won't subside
Days with endless fears
Eyes with silent tears
As he learned his best friend died
Fighting to be free
For all the world to see
Human life should be this way
A country with suppression
Her people lost in depression
Cannot go on another day
Liberty is in the sky
No more the children cry
As love escaped the heart
One world eternally united
A future not to be divided
Humans together nevermore apart

No more the children will cry
For freedom he gives his life

Mine to Give

All that is me with you I share
If you want Heaven I'll take you there
If I had the ability
To gather the stars
Then the universe I'd give to you
If Heaven was mine
To give to one person
You'd be the one I'd choose
If the clouds in the sky
Were making you sad
I'd blow them all away
If words were needed
To make you smile
I'd search for the ones to say
If you needed someone
To listen to your thoughts
This much I know I could do
If you need someone
To just hold and love
I'm always here for you

Wings of an Angel

Ride as one in unison,
Amongst natures beautiful things,
Ride as one for a purpose,
As an angel gets her wings,
Forgive all the pain,
And sorrow left behind,
Ride as one together,
Celebrate life just one more time,
Ride with hands joined,
As she smiles from Heaven's Gate,
Her wings in beautiful bloom,
The world accepting her fate,
Her love will never die,
It will guide you through it all,
Ride on the wings of an angel,
Ride again never to fall,
We'll meet again in Heaven,
You're forever in our dreams,
Know that we will miss you,
As we lay our love upon your wings.

Immunity Lost

There is no hiding from what is real
Regardless of the pain it makes you feel
The cards you're dealt are yours to keep
There is no healing of wounds so deep
They stay inside your heart, within your soul
Leaving no place to run, nowhere to go
Dreams become nightmares, a mind in despair
The visions never fade, seen everywhere
A heart grows cold, hatred dares win
Darkness falls, schizophrenia sets in
This road traveled, speeding, no brakes
Detours abound, yet all appear fake
The brain screams, a heart with sorrow
Wishing to sleep, well past tomorrow
Tired eyes wide open, memories cease to rest
No preparation, for this ruthless test
Strength begins to wither, fear supersedes
Another day, night, another heart bleeds
What is here, is without technicality
Time to realize, no immunity from reality.

America

To the sea there's many a mountain,
A sky ever so blue,
Freedom within her pastures,
Love that can't be more true,
Heavenly in her posture,
A touch as gentle as can be,
Harmony whispering in her winds,
Tis the land of the free,
Think of her as you choose,
For she'll love you any way,
Never to turn her back,
Nor take her beauty away,
Respect her with your heart,
Her beauty is forever,
She'll take you on her journey,
Hand in hand, always together,
Fill your eyes with her pictures,
As the memories enter your mind,
It's then you'll truly realize,
America is beautifully one of a kind.

A heavenly angel
With a Godly smile
You take my breath away
You've set my world
On a loving spin
My heart beats faster each day
Love can be strange
It can be blind
But with you the world will see
True love is out there
Waiting to be found
You only must believe
I love you so much
And it makes me wonder
Why a fool I was before
It was all a lesson
I needed to learn
So I could love you more

Within the stars a plan was born
The Angels harmony began to chime
The two of them became one
The day you became mine

Somewhere off in a distant place
Someone awoke a jaded heart
They knew this was just the beginning
Of something meant never to part

The world turns peaceful, the sun shines brighter
A bird's song echoes through the air
Even nature seems to know
When something is meant to be shared

I wake each day, new senses alive
Finally feeling how love can be true
I dream at night and I realize
How lucky I am to have you

From deep within, my love is yours
From now until forever
I surrender my heart into your arms
Two hearts, one love together

You

You are beautiful
You are pretty
You are wonderful
You hold my heart
You make me smile
You make me warm
You make me a better person
My world turns so much differently
All because of you
I love you

How Beautiful I Think You Are

You could light my world
If the sun's fire began to fade
You give me hope for tomorrow
As I walk through today
You show me love has meaning
Each time I look into your eyes
You give a spark to the stars
In my once darkened skies
Because of you, I feel alive
My heart beats brand new
I wake each day with internal smile
Because of the beauty that is you.

You Are the Reason

You are the reason
I smile in the morning
You are the reason
I dream at night
You are the reason
The rain stopped pouring
You are the reason
My future is right
You are the reason
Behind the meaning of my heartbeat
You are the reason
For a life so new
You are the reason
The world will see
All of the reasons
I fell in love with you

My sky is not blue,
My will can't pull me through
I wish I could cry
I wish I could die
I wish this life was through
Reflections in the wind
An unforgivable sin
I've lost my might
Lost the fight
Lost the desire to win
I bow my head in shame
Can no longer withstand the pain
My heart cannot heal, cannot feel
Cannot find the reason again
My soul ungracefully gone
It held on for so long
It has nothing left to live
Nothing left to give
Nothing left to move on
Please shed no more tears
Or succumb to your fears
It was there all along
It was bound to become too strong
It was meant to happen for years
At least I can say I tried
Through all the tears I've cried
Time to accept my fate
Time can no longer wait
Time is no longer on my side

Nothing grips you more
Stronger than before
Taking your breath away,
Emotional desire
Fates eternal fire
Upon the need our hearts we lay,

Dreams becoming real
Feelings that we feel
Life begins from here,
A child's first breath
A father giving way to death
An emotion to conquer the fear,

A soul coming alive
A reason behind the drive
The definition of our heart,
Releasing to be free
From within we finally see
The light shining in the dark,

Illuminating the way
Illusions gone away
Love and peace as one,
Hand in hand together
Leading the way to forever
Life has begun.

Dream

We close our eyes to visions
That play upon a mind at rest,
Viewing secrets held within
Fulfilling our hearts quest,

Carried into our waking moments
Episodes of Déjà vu,
Seeking to separate all that's fantasy
Yearning for what is true,

Faith holds the key to the doors
Locked behind your eyes,
Hope has the answers to a soul's desire
To silence midnight cries,

Trust the words your mind will speak
As yesterday drifts away,
Tomorrow's light will brightly shine
Bringing promise to a brand-new day.

Nature exhales
Sending a feather
Drifting through the air,
She smiles
At what she has done
Knowing her presence is everywhere,

Mountains stand
Tall above the shadows
Displaying beauty for all to see,
Mighty and proud
A show of strength
A symbol of all that is free,

The ocean's blue
Waves crash ashore
Mightily without sound,
Washing away
Wishes upon the sand
For another day to be found,

The earth spins
Around its light
Giving promise to all that dream,
For the courage
To conquer fear
To hold on to what we believe.

Sacred eternity waits within its wings,
Only to be found when the soul sings,
She does not hide knowing she's your desire,
A heart must be pure to feel her fire,
When she's found, she lives to her name,
Eternal peace and love never again the same,
Her smile brings life, her presence grace,
Her beauty surely to take your breath away,
Tell her your desires, tell her your needs,
Share your dreams, tell her what you see,
Share with her what makes you cry,
Open your soul, let her inside,
It's then that her touch will dry the rain,
Only then can love heal the pain.

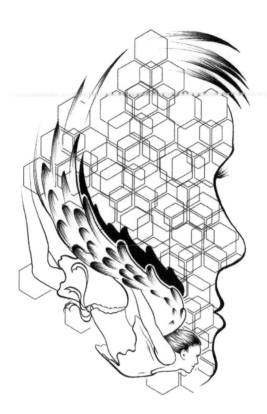

Evanescence

Her pale blue vision
Filled with shadows
Of evaporating time,
The final orange glow
Slowly fades away
Without reason to its rhyme,

A jet-black sea
Millions of candles
Attempting to be the guide,
As another one goes
Another is near
Setting the stage for her colors to collide,

Her presentation can be timed
Like clockwork in the sand
Her beauty for all to see,
She displays without prejudice
Her charming ability
To show that all is free.

Her smile,
An aura it shall change,
Her eyes,
Within you'll drift away,
Her hair,
Flowing as nature is free,
Her beauty,
Beyond what your eyes can see,
Her passion,
Taken for granted until now,
Her promise,
To save her heart somehow.

Answer

Can you find love
Without peace of mind?
Is there peace of mind in love?
In a world full of lust and greed
In a reality of push and shove,

Our hearts are taught
To search for love
Our minds calculate for peace,
Can we survive, without one or the other?
Are both needed to be free?

In the end
We may never know
The answers to our desires,
From now til then, we'll play the game
Praying to not be burned by the fire.

Close your eyes
Inhale
Gather today's trials inside,
The pain
The anger
The fear
All the tears you've cried,

Bring it all together
So you
Can view it one last time,
The fight
The agony
The defeat
The hopelessness that it defines,

Open your eyes wide
Exhale
Release them from your mind,
The weight
The world
The walls
Leave them all behind.

The Cardinal

Through a spirit's wish
It's perched above
To bring upon
A message of love
From well beyond
This life we know
To show in loss
That love still grows
At the darkest depths
Of pain filled sorrow
Here to remind you
There will be tomorrow
Listen closely
As the cardinal sings
To the comfort
That he brings
Feel inside
It's meant to be
He came to you
To remember me.

Me Too

As the numbers started to grow,
Memories rushed back to mind,
To let anyone know,
She wasn't sure if it was the time,

Headlines reaching the masses,
Men of power began to fall,
Their actions deemed classless,
Millions together standing tall,

With each new day, a new name,
Displayed for the world to see,
She felt she'd be blamed,
So full of uncertainty,

A secret kept inside,
She's held on to for so long,
To get back the part of her that died,
Taken by his actions, so wrong,

Will she find the courage to share,
Will she be able to pull through,
Will she finally find a voice that cares,
When she finally says "me too?"

Pipeline

All in the name of power,
For the desire to build greed,
Fictitious stories about safety,
Lies about what we need,

Through sacred land you wish to march,
With your iron vehicles of death,
Her people will stand, they will fight,
Until their final breath,

You won't contaminate our precious water,
You can't desecrate our burial grounds,
We'll fight your lies, your abuse of power,
We are one, standing tall, standing proud.

The day started normal,
Same routine,
Same old thing,
Just like the day before,
No one could predict,
Life would change,
Never be the same,
Will not see their smile anymore,

As they set out with smiles and dreams,
Innocence lost,
Life's greatest cost,
Because someone's heart turned to stone,
No one knew that day,
World's shattered,
Heart's tattered,
Their child was never coming home,

We need to find our souls,
This isn't right,
We must fight,
To show the love inside our heart,
We must save our children,
Good or bad,
Happy or sad,
It's us where it needs to start.

You

Each day we look for answers,
To the questions we hold inside,
For ways to make a difference,
To live a better life,

We listen to the experts,
Build trust in words spoken,
Caught inside a vicious circle,
A society living so broken,

Take a look inside,
It's there where it needs to start,
We are the reason for what we see,
For our world being torn apart,

If we want answers we must realize,
No other place can change come true,
Nothing else can make it happen,
Peace and love begin with you.

Waking up
Eyes closed tight
I'm here not there
Something doesn't seem right

Yesterday the sky
Above me was blue
Now all has gone dark
Can't remember what I knew

It's the one thing
We're taught from first breath
If you live this life
You'll have to accept death

We're at the mercy
Of Nature's time clock
No chance to stop the clicking
All we hear is tick tock

So as I woke this morning
Into a world I never knew
I finally realized
My life there was through

Sometimes
Understanding
Failure
Finally
Opens
Channels
Around
That
Inspire
Ones
New path.

Let go
Let breathe
Let love
Be free

Alissa

One night I wished upon a star,
A wish destined to come true,
One which was born inside my heart,
A wish that I'd find you,

One night I dreamt a lifelong dream,
One that has never felt so real,
Something closer than it ever seemed,
Feelings I never believed I'd feel,

One day I prayed I'd feel your love,
So that my life would be complete,
I reached out to those above,
To bring your heart to me,

One morning I woke and there you were,
Lying by my side,
I never doubted, was never unsure,
Leaving fate to be the guide,

Prayers answered, a wish granted,
All my dreams come true,
On a clear night, a shooting star planted,
In my heart my love for you.

Peace of Mind

When you find it
Your heart knows it's true,
It gives the way
In all that you do,
It shines its light
From the darkness you see,
You feel with your soul
What's meant to be,
With every breath
Every beat of your heart,
Every dream
Defines who you are,
When you live it
When it makes you blind,
It's only then
Peace of mind.

CPSIA information can be obtained
at www.ICGtesting.com
Printed in the USA
FSHW012019200819
61263FS

9 780359 450916